Reptile World

Sea Snakes

by Vanessa Black

Bullfrog
Books

Ideas for Parents and Teachers

Bullfrog Books let children practice reading informational text at the earliest reading levels. Repetition, familiar words, and photo labels support early readers.

Before Reading

• Discuss the cover photo. What does it tell them?

• Look at the picture glossary together. Read and discuss the words.

Read the Book

• "Walk" through the book and look at the photos. Let the child ask questions. Point out the photo labels.

• Read the book to the child, or have him or her read independently.

After Reading

• Prompt the child to think more. Ask: Have you ever seen a sea snake? Was it wild or in a zoo?

Bullfrog Books are published by Jump!
5357 Penn Avenue South
Minneapolis, MN 55419
www.jumplibrary.com

Library of Congress Cataloging-in-Publication Data

Names: Black, Vanessa, author.
Title: Sea Snakes / by Vanessa Black.
Other titles: Bullfrog books. Reptile world.
Description: Minneapolis, MN: Bullfrog Books, [2017]
Series: Reptile world
Audience: Ages 5–8. | Audience: K to grade 3.
Includes index.
Identifiers: LCCN 2016002939
ISBN 9781620313855 (hardcover: alk. paper)
Subjects: LCSH: Sea snakes—Juvenile literature.
Classification: LCC QL666.O64 B53 2017
DDC 597.96/5—dc23
LC record available at http://lccn.loc.gov/2016002939

Editor: Jenny Fretland VanVoorst
Series Designer: Ellen Huber
Book Designer: Lindaanne Donohoe
Photo Researcher: Lindaanne Donohoe

Photo Credits: Alamy, 5, 6–7, 14–15, 20–21, 23bl; Biosphoto, 18–19, 23tr; Corbis, 3; Getty, 9, 10–11, 12, 14 (inset), 16–17; National Geographic, 22; Nature Picture Library, 1, 24; Ruchira Somaweera, cover; Shutterstock, 4, 13, 17 (inset), 23tl, 23br; SuperStock, 8.

Printed in the United States of America at Corporate Graphics in North Mankato, Minnesota.

No.

It is a sea snake!

A sea snake is a reptile.

It has lungs.

It breathes air.

How does it live
in the sea?

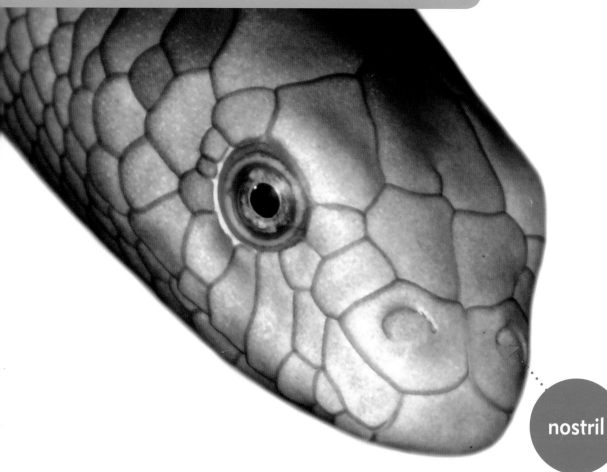

It has nostrils that shut.
No water can get in.

nostril

It can stay underwater
a long time.

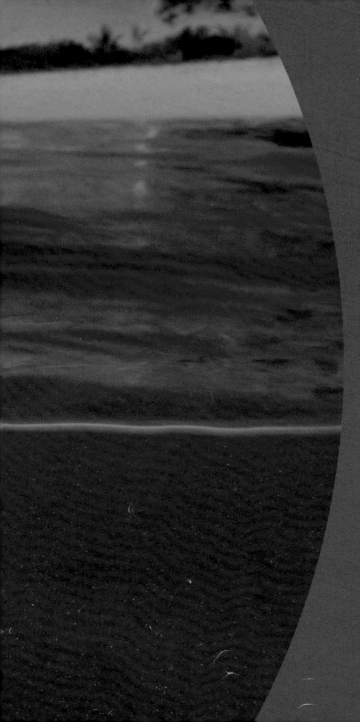

This sea snake
needs air.

She swims up
to breathe.

This snake is hungry.

He sees a fish.
Can he catch it?

He moves his flat tail.
It helps him go fast.

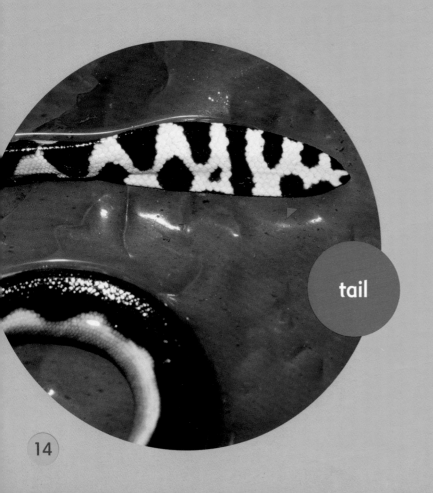

tail

He grabs the fish.

His fangs inject venom.

The fish dies.

Gulp!

venom

Look! This snake shed his skin.

Sea snakes shed a lot.

Now he is sleek.

He swims off
in his new skin.

Swish!

Parts of a Sea Snake

fangs
Most sea snakes
are poisonous.
They inject venom
through hollow fangs.

tail
A sea snake has a flat,
paddle-like tail.

skin
Sea snakes have smooth
skin. It helps them glide
through the water.

patterns
Many snakes have
patterns on their
bodies. Some snakes
have rings or spots.

Picture Glossary

lungs
The organs that animals and people use to breathe air.

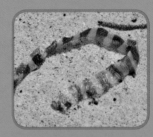
shed
To lose old skin.

reef
A shallow place in the ocean where there are corals and long lines of rocks.

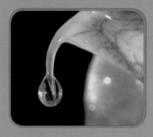
venom
Poison.

Index

To Learn More

Learning more is as easy as 1, 2, 3.

1) Go to www.factsurfer.com

2) Enter "seasnakes" into the search box.

3) Click the "Surf" button to see a list of websites.

With factsurfer.com, finding more information is just a click away.